BREATH

Author:
Deborah Boynes
© 2023 -2024

Layout and Design Artist:
Kelvin Thomas
kelvinjthomas@gmail.com

Editor:
Pat John-Baptiste

Proofreader:
Dominic John-Baptiste

Graphics by Canva

All rights reserved. No part of this book may be used, reproduced, translated, adapted, transformed, publicly performed, stored in a retrieval system, communicated to the public or transmitted in any form or by any means, electronic, mechanical, photocopying, recording, or otherwise, without the express permission of the author.

ENDORSEMENT

Walk into a garden that vibrates with inviting poetic rhythms from across the globe; a paradise that pulses with every colour of life - from the childhood colours of an enchanting little 'Hopping Bird' to the bold hues of youth in 'Friend Zone' and 'Shyness Trap', to the darkening shades of ageing hands in 'Those Hands.' Explore. Let the beauty of prosody, of poesy, elevate your soul to a place where you can **Breathe ... Alive!**

Walk into the shade of an umbrella of Grace, Light, Hope and Healing. Curl up in your favourite reading nook with this beautiful, and beautifully-crafted creation, and **Breathe ... Alive!**

- Pat John-Baptiste

I always knew that Deborah was a poet, but now I have seen her talent on full display in this piercing collection of poetry, **Breathe ... Alive**. *"Adolescent Angst" was just one of the poems that made me think, "How did Deborah know how I felt?" and then at other times, "But really, how does she know?"*

I came to anticipate what was in a poem before I read it. It was liberating to see those parts of myself in poetry and letting go.

- Marcia Headley

ACKNOWLEDGEMENT

I am thankful for the people who made **Breathe … Alive** *eminently better than I could have done.*

This includes Pat John-Baptiste, my editor, who guided and encouraged me to finish my manuscript. Also, I cannot forget my niece, Johanna Jordan, who conceptualised the front cover of **Breathe … Alive***.*

November 20, 2024

DEDICATION

To *my nieces and nephews,
who were always excited and gracious as I sharpened my art of
storytelling on them throughout their childhood.*

And to *my special friends, including Camille and Pat
who inspired me to produce* **Breathe ... Alive!**

TABLE OF CONTENTS

1.	**BREATHE ALIVE**
2.	*Breathe Alive*
3.	**IMPRESSIONS**
5.	*To Catch a Bashful Hopping Bird*
6.	*Refresh*
7.	*Time in Stasis*
9.	*Anarchy*
11.	*The Lindi*
13.	*Island*
15.	*Shadow*
17.	*In Your Friend Zone*
19.	*Surface Depth*
21.	**EXCAVATION – BENEATH THE OUTER CORE**
23.	*Adolescent Angst*
27.	*Home*
29.	*Original Pain*
32.	*Padded Prison*
35.	**LYRICAL TALES**
37.	*Those Hands*
	Part I
	Part II
40.	*The Night*
41.	*Stalker-ish: Pride Ushering a Fall*
	Part I
	Part II
	Part III
	Part IV
45.	*Adolescence – Shyness Trap*
47.	**SALUTATIONS**
49.	*A Dance into Your Ecosystem*
50.	*Burning Bright*
51.	*You Are More*
52.	*Climb*
53.	**SONG OF TRINIDAD**
55.	*Inverse Parallel Realities*

TABLE OF CONTENTS

57.	**RIDDLES**
60.	*A Taste of Retro Vintage Toco*
	Riddle One
	Riddle Two
	Riddle Three
	Riddle Four
	Riddle Five
62.	*Across Continents*
	Riddle One
	Riddle Two
	Riddle Three
	Riddle Four
	Riddle Five
63.	**ORIENTAL BREEZE**
64.	*Golden Tears*
64.	*Freedom's Call*
64.	*Hope Awaiting*
65.	**INSPIRATION**
66.	*No More Flying Monkeys*
67.	*Avian Oxymoron*
69.	**PIECES OF POETRY:** *Particles of Philosophy*
71.	*Serene*
71.	*Defiant Courage*
71.	*Undying Courage*
71.	*Constancy*
72.	*Chicken Hope*
72.	*Shield of Authenticity*
72.	*The Taste of Truth*
72.	*Insistent Splendour*
73.	*A Taste of Retro Vintage Toco - Answers*
76.	*Across Continents - Answers*
77.	**GLOSSARY OF TERMS**
79.	**ABOUT THE AUTHOR**

BREATHE ... ALIVE

1 | *Breathe ... Alive*

Breathe ... Alive

*Our soul lies unborn and asleep
until we erupt from the chrysalis
of the restraint of fear
... and it flutters
as we metamorphose
and breathe alive
in the beauty of daylight
... growing stronger wings
borne aloft on the winds
en route to Destiny!*

IMPRESSIONS

The impact of the passage of time is a gravitational pull on the thrill and wonderment at our achievements, social experiences and possessions
... so defy mental gravity –

Breathe ... Alive!

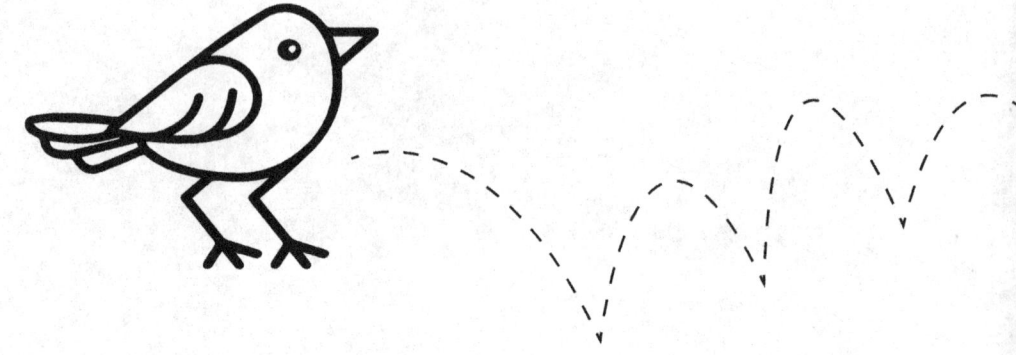

To Catch ...

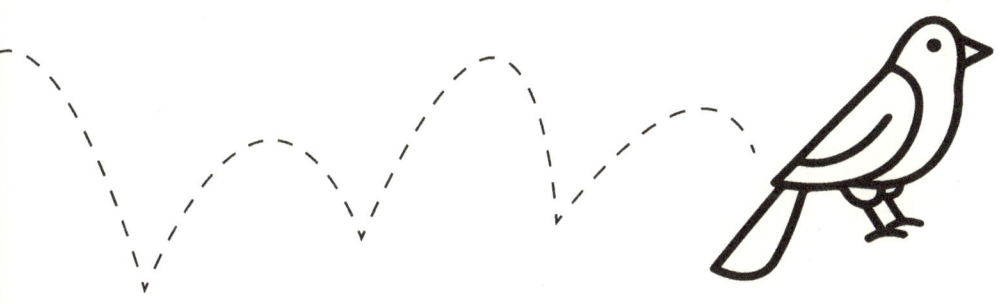

... a Bashful Hopping Bird

*You hop around me
…
then you're gone
in an elusive dance.*

*You flitter close
You escape me
You trail me
You derail me
You enthral me
Leaving me riveted
Thoroughly fascinated
Profoundly
    disappointed
I remain … somewhat distracted.*

*I wait
to see you in flight
Painful delight
A joyous plight
Until I'm bold enough to stay still
while you survey me
and you're not afraid
nor am I afraid
to greet you.*

Refresh

*The facets of your
cobalt eyes beam
splendorous light
of diamond stars
– inset on the curtain
of a cloudless night –
with all that's good,
wondrous and bright
and usher in
the warming sight
of the dawning of
your stellar smile!*

Time in Stasis

*You've touched me
... deeply ... profoundly
like crimson dye
staining the
synapses of my brain.
Beyond your
vivacity
poise
and acuity
I'll remember the
grace in you, and the beauty!*

*As evenings vow to chase the days
waves recede against sunlit shores
time erodes the rock of life and
reduces its might to grains of sand
there will remain a trace of you!*

*Should geriatric-fugue befog my mind
a precise sketch of your soft hand
would be imprinted on my emotions
so my soul shall remember you.*

*Were we to exist for ten lifespans
or ever depart each other's orbits
for one thousand years in time
– as would a friendly ship salute
exuberant shouts of castaways –
when we do collide
I will surely remember you.*

To my lovely friend, Pat, who trained me to see beauty in the ashes!

Anarchy

*You've resiled
from all that's
engagingly insidious.*

*Imperfect beauty
Incongruent harmony
Innocent sagacity
Impregnable frailty
Anti-systemic ...
Running along a fault line.*

*Anarchist beauty
Anarchist security
Anarchist harmony
Anarchist sincerity
Cuts the dark in two
It's safe to feel with you
... to be with you.
I'm drawn to you.*

The Lindi

Smile nah!
Crack your lips
just ... a little bit!
Erect a floodgate
for repugnance and horror
pouring through your pores
at all intransigent stupidity
at unmitigated insanity!

Try smiling nah!
Like for real!
You've flailed and failed
to tether your thoughts
... to only produce the smile
of the carcass of a roasted
dog with a frozen toothy grin
in the noonday sun!
Corral serene thoughts within
– tranquillise your brain –
relieve the abrasion of vacuity!

*You bleed your thoughts
with cosmic speed
of an unruly racehorse
cantering pell-mell out
the stable and down a cliff
– beyond the reach of recall!
… and are mocked
with the irony of your shock
at unmitigated imbecility
that sedates your brain
when rebukes are apt.*

*… alas! Comebacks crystallise
a decade later.*

*To my dearest friend, Lindi, who laughs with me at my failed
attempts to don a poker face, and whose kind words inspire me
to see that the best response to all levels of madness is to focus
on what is good and beautiful.*

Island

*Time to HeaL
Time to grOW
exhume your fears
then let them GO
to be you, to GLow
and to KnoW
the unique pattern
of your inner design
radiates
slivers of light –
slender, silken and bright.*

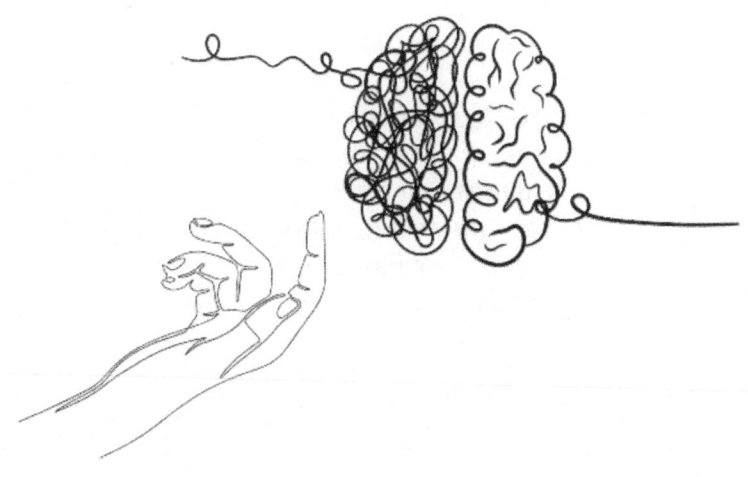

So ... it's time
to ShoW
your layers of fabric
to the right ones
at the right times
and to spring
over the boundary
of any doubt that
– although you live
on a lone island
of peculiar and enchanting
thoughts in your head
in a language you
can only speak to yourself
never traced on a map
... and perhaps can't be found –
when you do Pourrrrr
a drink of
your je ne sais quoi
originality
from the depths
of your SElf
you enamour
folks who savour
and deeply cherish
its distinct flavour
which can intensify
if you become an ally of the truth ...
that your inner side
is worthy of display.

Shadow

*All I see of you
is stilted ...
like a starched robe
you never take off
to let me view
your iconic style of dress
...
engendering intrigue
of what's beneath
and behind
your well-honed
unnaturally unwavering
Ms. Universe smile.*

*We sit
and fellowship
in this gazebo
– a shallow communion –
the banquet table seats
at which you serve feasts
of your thoughts
are occupied by
non-extant friends.*

*... so I halt at the door
of your house
where lights are dim
and I'm never let in.*

*Everything you are
is the reflection of light
from a dead star
that shone
a million years ago*

and
your expressions
of a moon somewhat dim
– projecting splintered
rays
from the sun
of your fractured soul.

It's only W
      h
        e
          n
you'd be so bolD
to perceive and regard
– with entirety –
all within your mind, heart and soul
… and fall into honesty with yourself
and the rest of the world
I could see you
… clearly …
as a whole!

In Your Friend Zone

I stoked a blaze for you
A raging flambeau ....
standing by my window
hoping I could see yours
flicker back like a beacon to me
... a blaze ... doused with blackouts of communication
your forgetfulness of my existence
like intermittent showers
but too regular
then later resuscitated with your pleas:
I'm sorry!

I am a mere flicker of a glimpse
of a shadow of your afterthoughts
... Like a photo retrieved from a dusty box
to quell your boredom when excitement sleeps
on slow weekends!

Calcified and comatose emotional organs
dead to vulnerability of intimacy
lie behind your skeletal frame of bravado
under the skin of your sociability!
Your kind smiles are a porous cloak ...
an inept and cosmically failed antidote
against the niggling bitter and biting reality –
the joyous weighty warmth of my regard for you
is intensely burdensome
for me!

Breathe ... Alive

*My flame flickered into embers so molecular
in my clarity
like electric sparks of a nebula
against the tapestry of a keen moon
wearing a gown with a train of the clear night skies
and sprinkled with a string of twinkling stars
bearing a crystalline light of the gift of love
I should give to myself
and one day to a beautiful soul
who brandishes a torch for me!*

Surface Depth

It's just my skin;
it hasn't written me in ink
or even graphite – pencil –
etching me in a permanent pen
Your self-manufactured goggles
impose on me
your intrusively concocted camouflage.
You don't see or feel ME
– concealed –
behind the skin I'm in.

The skin I'm in
peach, ivory or mocha cream –
you believe confines me
to be a thief, a saint, a sinner,
shady, helpless, invincible, affluent
or an unredeemable bottom feeder!
You assume,
I'm Mensa quality intellectual or
an empty skull,
its walls ricocheting echoes of nothing!
Minus Zero cranial capacity!

Veins throb with blood
below the skin I'm in.
Pumping oxygen mingled
with malice, rot, rage and rancour,
beauty, hope or relentless courage,
underneath my skin!

It's just
layers
of
fabric
… encasing
who
I
am
This thin skin which I'm in!

EXCAVATION – BENEATH THE OUTER CORE

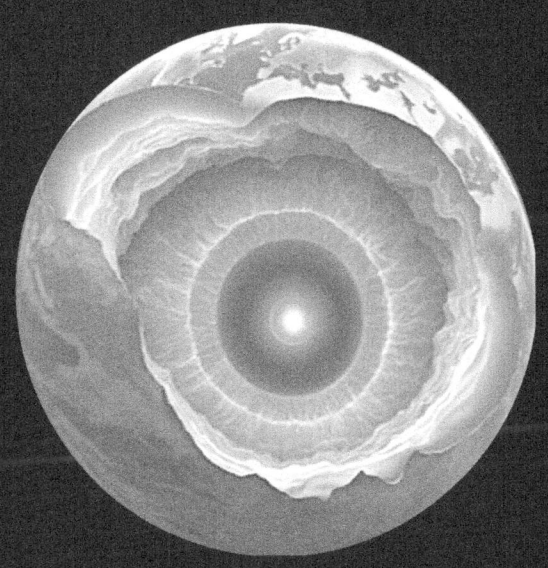

Poetry could be a thing of beauty, simply in its form. Poetry becomes true artistry when it mirrors the sharpness, depths and inflections of the human experience.

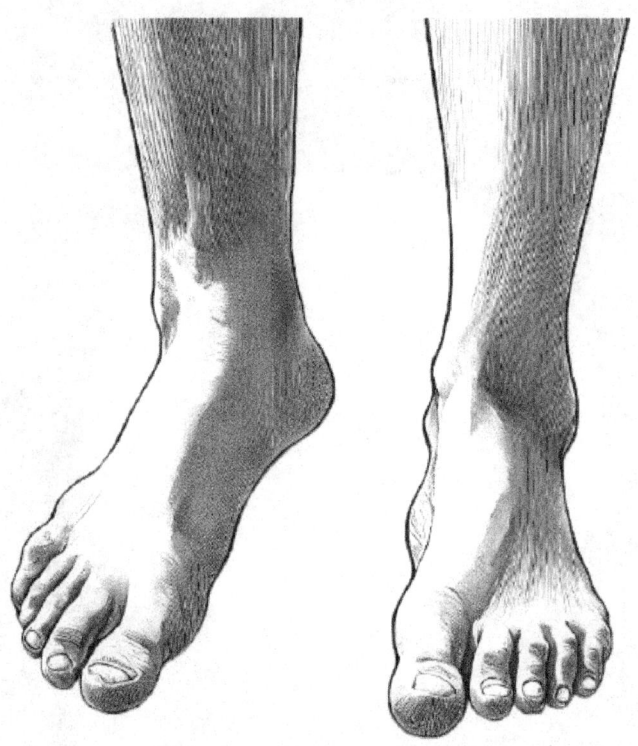

Adolescent Angst

Me ...
I exist.
Doubting I'm alive.
I'm light gas
filling the vacancy in a room
– the lull of conversations –
with raspy laughs.
I mimic smiles
and facial reactions
... like an imposter
... an extra-terrestrial alien.
I falter at being human.

To the world
I doubt that I'm alive.
What's my shape,
my outline and my profile?
Sometimes a bird ...
I fly on the wind of compliments
then plummet to self-doubt,
all in a single swoop.

My heart palpitates
at a stranger's minute glance.
I flounce with pride.
Eyes raze me!
They scrutinise
my pimpled-speckled face!
I win the battle of my will
– refuse to wither in their gaze –
but then capitulate!

I stumble when I walk.
My hodgepodge personality
– the prisoner in me –
stands behind bars ... peeping
in adult clothes and shoes
... not fitting:
like a zombie
in healthy human skin
but bloodless!
I'm a vampire in the stark sun.
I need to run!

I shiver in a coat of fear
– of flimsy furry warmth
and infiltrating bony chill –
fatiguing!
A sun-starved plant
… I pine for light
release from blistering blight
– dread of dissection –
this self-inflicted plight!
… But,
my strength simply snoozes –
      g
    n
  i
sprout
      tendrils –
just in sight!

I stretch.
I strain.
I scour.
Like probing restless roots.
Undeterred!
Resolute!
Daring the mirror image –

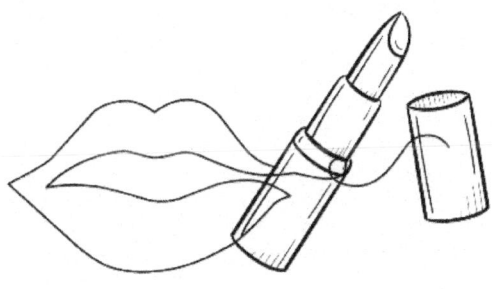

25 | Breathe … Alive

Me:
Quit quaking ... cease vacillating
on a pendulum of vaporosity
and solidity
... and merge with me
the contemporary!
Then I'll dance
in step with me.
In a dress of my
permanent skin.
A sturdier configuration:
Me!

Home

An unallayed deluge of tears
can vanquish your retentive fears.
Race ... undeterred ...
down an alley
banked ...
flanked
by feral thoughts
– famished pot-hounds –
barking!
Tame them
along the boardwalk of restoration.
Take your thoughts
Home!

Rouse your soul from synthetic-fragile
peace born in a restless
Cause!
Pause!
Kidnap your thoughts ...
that skylark in tropical antics:
vacillation from half-sunny skies
to thunderous rain
and
Let them Sit ...
in your head's quiet chapel
– a verdant coverage
ensconced in rustling bamboo leaves –
scarfed by a river singing silent hymns
until ...
they settle down
at HOME with you!

*There ...
wrestle with passing angels
and wrest from them the oil of peace.
Bless your heart!
Inhale the innocent breath
of child-like wonder,
unreserved exploration
and unrestricted fascination
with the World and your Thoughts
on the way HOME to you!*

Original Pain

*I greet me
in my shattered childhood.
I harvest the fragments
I grieve for what I lost
and never gained –
vulnerable wonderment
at life
every minute movement
of butterflies taking flight.
Not afraid to f*
a
 l
  l.

*Fear is a strange relative.
The world is a beautiful garden
– where snakes smile and grant kisses –
for discovery!*

*I acquit those that broke my beads of glass
who burnt away my warmth of toys
the joy of play and thrill of games
hauled me outside
to peer at dreary clouds
kept me a prisoner of my insides
way before my Minor Mind was ripe
to see anything but sunny skies.*

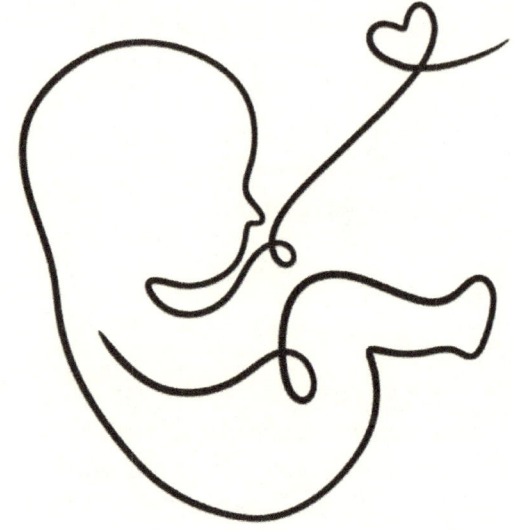

*I relinquish pain of
unconscious hate
of myself
and the one who relegated me to a fate
to curl under a curtain
that draped my inner child with angst
like spooks …
that haunt my broken childhood.*

*I imbibe the full cup of wine
in all that's present – now – in time
to redeem the
squandered boon and bliss
of childhood.
I embrace and imbue
this child –
drowning in an oversized
cloak
of
… pain –
with the warmth
of healing
through gentle kisses
from a Mended Me,
in farewell to my broken childhood.*

Padded Prison

She died and woke up
trapped inside of him …
in his love – a padded prison.
A seedy and sullied paradise.
Captive in her Eden with Satan's serpent
each day … deceiving!
Deceiving!

He's a cuddly Koala bear
with undertones of granite
embracing her
with his fiery hotness
… then bruising her
with anaesthetising cold.

His toxin is her oxygen.
Her prospect of independent
breathing – a suffocating gas –
carbon dioxide!
She's a tree with rotted roots.
Falling.
He chomps on each leaf
– her dreams –
like gluttonous bachac ants.
He invades her garden ... hiding
Camouflaging ... like green locusts
... leaving wizened blackened branches
... desiccated.

Behind closed doors
he serenades her at his feast
– overflowing with wine and lobsters –
gifts of Tiffany trinkets
and fresh flowers ...
later capsized in erratic rage!
She's pulverised with cuffs
and kicks.
He offers homage to her memento
– cuts and bruises – with soft kisses.
She favours her right side
– the site of her wounds!
Her psyche withers ...
but hope insulates her brain
from reality!
~~~
hope
"Wretched, wolverine, warped,
foul and long-fanged hyena!
Foolish man!"

I plead with her, "Here is the key.
He's a mirage … you're in the desert.
Here's a new space … a greenhouse.
You're in a dream!
Smoke's distorting your image
– in a splintered mirror –
Strrrrrrretch your hands into it
… like a test!
Regurgitate his poison –
liquefied Stockholm Syndrome pills!"
Sigh ….

She flees proximate rescue …
She remains rolling in her Mud
Clinging to him – her Pig!

The Toad!
She thinks
"He's bewitched, just for now!
I'll dilute this spell.
He'll resume the shape of my Prince …
Soon!"

The curse of his vileness remains.
He wields his own Dark Arts!
She's deaf to my music.
She can't hear my songs –
"You could walk free, Woman!
        P
         l
          e
           a
            s
             e!"

LYRICAL TALES

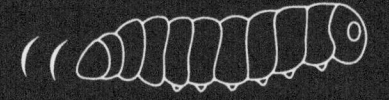

Music includes the rhythmic and sonorous song of poetry ... close your eyes and feel its beats!

Breathe ... Alive

The travelling bards of ancient cultures, West Indian calypsonians and other contemporary crooners have shown us that stories become memorable and beautiful when told through poetry and song. The art of storytelling was, and is, a capsule to share history, ideas and culture across generations.

Those Hands

Hmmm ... HANDs!
You think they're just that – simply hands?
Oh no! Your hands say so much about you.
Your hands record your stories!
Let me tell you a story about Raymond's hands.

Part I

Raymond's hands hold a story!
Their withered vein cupped pools of pain
that circulated through every inch of his body.
Their calluses stored his pungent sweat
of laborious days in the sweltering sun
with hands catching fish and mending nets
... hands working past sunset
– tirelessly – rebelling against starless nights
and unrelenting rain
... hands perpetually wrestling for a wage
... hands in a scurry as his hunger raged
... hands in a flurry of his pains to thrive
... hands in hurry as he strove to survive
... hands busy in a bustle to remain alive
... feverishly working hands!!

Raymond's wife surveyed his hands
with hard thoughts shooting from her eyes
"He waves about those useless hands
... constantly restless hands
which cannot meet a mere demand
to more than barely feed our little boy
with his hungry hungry eyes!"

Raymond's work was his sanctuary,
to which he was shackled by his hands.
Each night Raymond collapsed into bed
... always too late for the chance
to caress the cheeks of his son with
work-worn roughened hands
... though just in time for his wife to feign
deep sleep to escape the touch of his hands!

Part II

Raymond's hands expended energy
like burning wood on an altar of self-sacrifice
so that his golden son could
ascend above dark clouds of poverty
to the glorious sun of success.
Later ... through the toil of Raymond's hands
his son blossomed into an eminent doctor
... but, then ...
his son slowly evolved into stranger.
Raymond drank in the wonder of
shaking his son's soft and lotioned hands
about once a month ... then rarely ever
... then once a year ... and – finally – never!
Long after, as Raymond sat at a seaside
oblivious to the enchantment of the setting sun,
his crushed heart registered this rejection
while his hands stemmed a deluge ...
the flow of his tears ...
into
... hands perpetually wrestling for a wage
... hands in a scurry as his hunger raged
... hands in a flurry of his pains to thrive
... hands in hurry as he strove to survive
... hands busy in a bustle to remain alive
... those feverishly working hands!

38 | Breathe ... Alive

*Raymond's hands hold his story
marked by mental bruises and scars
more mangled than Mangrove tree roots.
Raymond now lies on a tattered pallet
on a street ... his fragile mind flails to recall
the warmth of a bed and house long gone
in a raging fire birthed by a felled lamp!
Raymond's feeble hands tug at a threadbare blanket
... too thin to warm his hands against
the cold of familial ingratitude
and soothe his
... hands that perpetually wrestled for a wage
... hands that scurried as his hunger raged
... hands once in a flurry of pains to thrive
... hands that hurried as he strove to survive
... hands once busy in a bustle to remain alive
... feverishly working hands!*

*Through unseeing eyes, Raymond pled for
a crumb of bread and raised his hands to me,
quivering with the weight of that story!
Those hands! Raymond's hands!*

The Night

My father said "Nights end too soon;
Dawn repels the stars and silver moon!"
But I shivered when daylight was done
and evenings eclipsed the golden sun!

I said, "At nights vile vampires are bold
They bark like dogs! They screech like owls!
They cry for blood and chill my soul!
They run about, they scream and howl!

My sister thought that nights are dressed
with floating cotton clouds where angels rest!
But once night struck, I slunk to bed
saying, "Ghosts could be real or in my head!"

Now my nights fade much too soon
when dawn's stark light invades my room
Noises of night like slow drum beats
now lull me into peaceful sleep!

Stalker-ish
Pride Ushering a Fall

Part I

*I rotated my torso and whipped my spindly arms
away from the iron grasp of his sweaty palms!
Any degree of curiosity on what he said
was entirely non-existent! Less than dead!
He wore the aura of a fetid sea fish
at the bottom of the 'normalcy bell curve': a Mr. Stalker-ish!*

*I rummaged through my purse, quivered and panted!
"Oh where are my car keys!" I repeatedly chanted
To repel the chills from a vivid image of me
asphyxiated, roped, with shattered knees:
trapped in the trunk of Mr. Stalkerish's car
and my mortal remains tossed in the Caroni river
like a Happy Meal snack for a ravenous cascadura:
an undignified death for me – a self-designated diva!*

*Hearing a crack under my feet, I pivoted around
and quickly looked down in chase of the sound.
"Oh there! My car keys are right on the ground!"
I snatched up the keys and squealed in joyous anticipation
of leaping into my car, being spurred into action
igniting my cold engine and feeling the warming satisfaction
of the fading chill of his cold memory:
Mr. Stalker-ish's zombie eyes, glued upon me!*

Part II

*His shadow pressed me like a crowbar!
So I yelped, recoiled and rolled onto the hood of my car.
"Hey Ma'am! Ma'am! Ma'am!
Please relax! Jeez! Just stay Calm!"*

Mr. Stalker-ish said with a shout
"I just wanted to tell you your shirt's turned inside out!"
Glancing at the inner seams poking from my white blouse
I assimilated what Mr. Stalker-ish was prattling about!
He smugly added, "Oh, and your front tyre is flat.
I'm assuming that you want help with that?"

I commenced a speedy calculation of the risks
and gauged the threat from this Mr. Stalker-ish!
Mr. Stalker-ish remained unnaturally still
like a panther paused and primed to make a kill
His eyes assaulted me with the feel of mossy slugs
slowly crawling out of my shirt, then plopping in the mud!
Mr. Stalker-ish was dressed in fairly robust clothing
several clicks above Rattans and other bargain-store offerings!
He had a sort of 'knock-off' Ted Bundy-serial killer finish.
But I had to take a chance with Mr. Stalker-ish!
So to dispatch our business with utmost speed
I eyed him in my peripheral vision and croaked, "Yes, please!"

Part III

I eyed him with impatience and dread
I repeatedly rotated my eyes a full axis into my head!
Eureka! He was then done and I was un-dead.
I hurriedly thanked him, averting my gaze
my discomfort evident, but he stood there unfazed.
I frantically slammed the door and started my car.
But did not escape hearing Mr. Stalker-ish whisper
"If you need to ...my name is M... uel ... ed!"
Whatever he thought remained unsaid
I escaped assassination and now had things to do!
I had to be punctual for my job interview!

I screeched into the parking lot of a partly burnt building
surrounded by lifeless ponds in need of refilling,

*It was an edifice deliberately and offensively ugly
adorned by a rusty sign stating, "Lester Law and Company",
hanging askew, tottering on the brink of annihilation,
like an appetiser prophesying an unpleasant meal to come!
The building screamed rat, cockroach and bat infestation
like a blaring horn, warning all to flee
from dreadful horrors one cannot forget or unsee!
I said to myself "I've been through too much today!
I rebuke you spidey sense: Just move out of my way!"
I scuttled into the building foyer and announced myself
my pouring perspiration just could not be helped.*

*The receptionist glared at me like a haughty fowl!
She struggled with the weight of a turtle-necked shroud
and inspected my blouse like the scorching beams of an alien ship
I interrupted her finite assessment, "I'd be back in a minute!"
I dashed to the washroom, hit my head on its door and stumbled,
"Dang! That 'Karen' had to see me at my worst!" I grumbled!*

Part IV

*I was shown a conference room cresting four flights of stairs,
with rotting boards inviting the unawares
way past their prime, solely for those nimble toes,
meandering past Jacob's ladder and steeper than Mt. Hololo!
I glanced at my watch. Oh no! I was two minutes late:
at the risk of the permanent taint of utter disgrace!
I raced up the stairs in my four-inch heels,
assured of a cat-like prowess to run with utter ease!*

*I was three feet away from the conference room door,
when one shoe-heel cracked and careened across the floor!
I emitted a shrill scream, a few octaves higher than a sow
birthing quadruplets or a soon-to-be slaughtered Christmas cow.*

Breathe ... Alive

*The door cracked open and I saw my death-wish:
snuggly observing me was none other than 'Mr. Stalkerish'!
He said, "I'm a partner here. We met this morning, for sure!
Now I have the pleasure of rescuing you once more …".*

*I glanced into the eyes of my stalker
my saviour
in keen pain
and saw staring at me
the stark and clear reflection
of my pride-fuelled … shame!*

Adolescence – Shyness Trap

Soft eyes transmute
to diamond-hard rock.
They emit a cold energy
– zapping my internal organs –
for one explosive second.
Across on the bleachers,
she inspects
a sun-bathed mango
in my hand
– not me –
studying them
… prepping
for a non-scheduled examination.
She's unaware of my eyes –
an MRI scanner.
I am an eighty-billionth
of a brain cell
outside the sphere
of her existence!

She swiftly skirts across
to my side of the field!
She sashays and spins
like a whirlwind
– around me –
and collides with her giggly friend
– behind me.
My cheeks preheat with shame.
I pluck invisible lint from my pants!

I glance at them both
in my periphery.
They walk off the field
Holding hands.
They turn, glimpsing back
and then skyward –
at a colourful kite …
not at me!
I'm temporarily empty!

I rouse myself.
The suave words
I should have said
Materialise – an hour later,
"Hey lovely lady! I'm Fred."
A template space-filler,
for further encounters.
Next time – the air in my lungs
will escape … like a wave
on my diaphragm
– pushing past the constipation
of words in my throat.
I'll do better!

SALUTATIONS

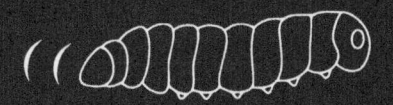

*Open our eyes to see each other as more than mere clutter –
Breathe ... Alive!*

48 | *Breathe ... Alive*

A Dance into Your Ecosystem

*Those who estimate their worth
with lesser weight than arid dirt
assign others with heavier currency
than self-existence, hence banished to be
unicellular parasites,
asphyxiating sapling trees!*

*You're a monumental palm
crowned by massive decorative fronds
stabilised by roots of self-love
deeply entrenched in the ground;
sourcing your own sustenance
while irradiating the air
with the incense
of your essence saturating
your sphere!*

Burning Bright

Burning bright for all to see is your blazing light,
a relentless bonfire, dispersing visceral obscurity of night,
pulsating sparks from a burnt tree of brittle mortality,
irradiating starless skies for pilgrims carving history.

You're a gentle wind riding the wake of a firestorm,
an enfolding strength of a house of hope, residing outside the norm.
Your tears soften the paths of co-travellers on knife-hard days,
to form a flaming road ahead, dismantling the smoky haze.

The light of your soul singing with fiery spirit-accompaniment,
pales the jewels adorning your tiara of accomplishments
effuses the soft air with the radiant triumph of your humility
and breathes an inferno to diffuse the cold heat of uncertainty.

A lighthouse which beckons us to kiss the shore one day
propelling us to find our way
is the keenness of your pure light,
burning bright for all to see,
which warms the hearts of seeking souls like me!

You Are More

You are more than the visible horizon of yourself.
Prise open the door to the sea of your mind!
Usher in flamboyant hope, a bold champion,
riding aloft a chariot of orange and fiery cotton clouds
which meld into the firm fist of a fearsome majestic God,
blast a ferocious roar to pulverise a road once disallowed
and hammer an expansive new mountain pass.

Trample on the unprecedented paths of the bold!
Scale beyond the fence, sail waves unwalled
and collapse off the edge of your world!
Delve deep within, past the fragile velvet-silkiness of soul
to the core of your steely spirit!
Shatter the prison mirror of a shadow-self
sweep away the fragments of fears you've felt.
Dare to breathe freely and strut in light
though initially startling and blindingly bright.
Reach into the depth of your essential core
... and evolve into more!

Climb

Climb your Mount Everest,
past the crest of clouds
causing you doubts,
and unfurl the pinnacles of your dreams!

Open your eyes to the dawning sun of your aspirations,
and the shining light of your
hopes, emerging
across a tapestry painting of your successes,
eclipsing
the grey glimmer of the moon!

Ruffle the feathers of your restless spirit.
Soar like a bird,
along the pathway
to the full evolution of your existence

Flap your wings
to an accompanying rhythm:
the beat of the stirrings in your heart!
Lest you flatline
to the eternal death of your psyche.

Heed the summons of your heart
Lift your eyes to the crown of your mountain
Ascend to new heights!
Elevate and evolve!
CLIMB!

SONG OF TRINIDAD

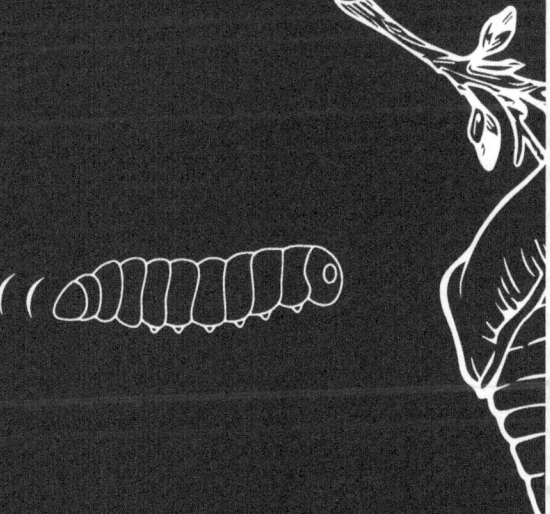

54 | Breathe ... Alive

Inverse Parallel Realities

She waves to her sister across the sea.
Her scent carries on the breeze over the hill,
… and she dances,
as you strum her song of Trinidad.

Strum beauty and diversity,
lush flora and fauna for miles to see!
Strum unique artistic creativity!
Strum intense and complex history!
Strum the song of Trinidad!

Strum away its pain and lies
brutal violence and maimed lives!
Strum away the heated fights!
Strum away the wake of mothers' agony!
Strum away bold and shameless robbery!

Beat the drum of Trinidad!
Beat to the pulse of Industry!
Beat to the buzz of businessmen!
Beat to the gurgle of rivers and streams!
Beat to the sound of birds in orange-gold skies!
Beat to the song of calypsos!
Beat to the rhythm of Chutney tunes!
Beat a welcome to scarlet ibis and white owls!
Beat away the smoke of littered streets!
Beat away the fog of the Beetham Dump
And the croaks of circling corbeaux above!

The song of Trinidad calls to me:
crab and callaloo on Sundays – calling me!
Sweet flesh of mango slices – calling me!
Melting textures of dasheen and dumplings – calling me!
Hot and heavy dry season – calling me!
From the cold of London and Paris – calling me!
From the Blue Mountains of Jamaica – calling me!
From the emerald isle of Barbados' idyll seas,
Calling me!

Noisy streets with chickens squawking – calling me!
Discordant clash of bustling cities with dense bushes, calling me!
Clicking forks on gourmet dishes – calling me!
Spicy aroma of pelau, doubles and roti – calling me!

Erudite scholars, debates and discussions,
Corralled by village gossip, in juxtaposition – calling me!
The struggle between despair and hope-filled exhilaration,
Calling me.
The sound of Trinidad is calling me!

RIDDLES

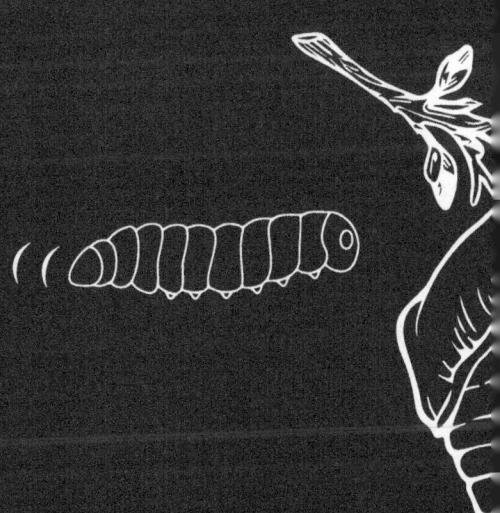

57 | *Breathe ... Alive*

58 | *Breathe ... Alive*

My mother grew up in the rustic town of Toco on the Island of Trinidad in the mid-1900s with simple technology.

As a child, my mother was introduced to a ripe tradition of storytelling and telling of riddles around fires on moonlit nights. This tradition was passed down to me and I am sharing a bit of it with you.

A Taste of Retro Vintage Toco

Riddle One

*Bring your cocoa tea, butter and knife
Aroma of coconut and nutmegs for spice
exuded from the fire above and beneath.*

Riddle Two

*You're green and round
hard like stone, tough like the ground
Good to store jewels, to hold a special dish
to carry water and to catch a crayfish.*

Riddle Three

*Like an ant mountain in the yard
A dome built of dirt, solid and hard
smoke flows from its lungs and over your head
dispersing the taste of crispy fresh bread.*

Riddle Four

*Wearing a hat of drooping fronds
its yellow fruits rain on the ground
Adorned with rows of lethal spikes -
a tree monkey know not to climb.*

Riddle Five

*At nights you tuck them into bed
With a sliding roof you cover their heads
Wake them up to bask in the daylight
Dance on their backs to make them bright.
Keep your eyes to the skies in case it rains -
for if they're ever drenched it's such a pain.*

Riddle answers on page 80

Across Continents

Riddle One:

*Twice a year
Distinct and rare
Earth steals the sky's light
and the moon cries blood.*

Riddle Two:

*Summer's special wear
Mayhaps just once a year
The sun kisses the moon
and the moon swallows the sun.*

Riddle Three:

*Sudden sprout of Spring –
Sown with joy and yielded in pain
The nestling's cries ... daily refrains.*

Riddle Four:

*Loud claps fill the night
– water splashed above my head
eyes are silent peace.*

Riddle answers on page 83

ORIENTAL BREEZE

When we pen a haiku, we package the monumental, intense and dense experiences that resonate with us into a tiny gift box ... so that none of the fine details, mystery, majesty and memories are lost in time.

Golden Tears

*Blooming poui trees –
flogged by thunder and showers
weeping gold flowers.*

Freedom's Call

*Swells of monsoon floods –
sail a river of freedom
Hope boldly beckons.*

Hope Awaiting

*Dormant wintry trees –
hibernating ambitions
snores until it's Spring.*

INSPIRATION

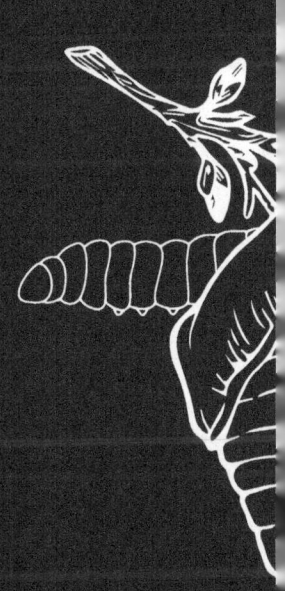

No More Flying Monkeys

Troops, rowdy circus,
marauding missiles, besiege the mind.
Hopeless mental regurgitation!

Past has passed,
simians shrieking, "We're not leaving!"
Piercing windows, frailty.

Peace, epaulettes adorning
raucous clawing monkeys, now disbanded
The stumble: the lie!

Avian Oxymoron

Fumbling 'yard-fowl'.
Foppish and fawning, failed façade!
Scrounging for worms, unyielding yard.

Feeble flutters, unctuous feathers!
Perching, preening and prepping for scooping
ejected victuals from passers-by!

The sun's rousing,
rays rebounding, splintered on white-specked quills.
Majestic ink-eyed hawk awaking!

Swoops down to conquer;
soaring above the yawn of day!
Trailing the stirs of hapless preys!

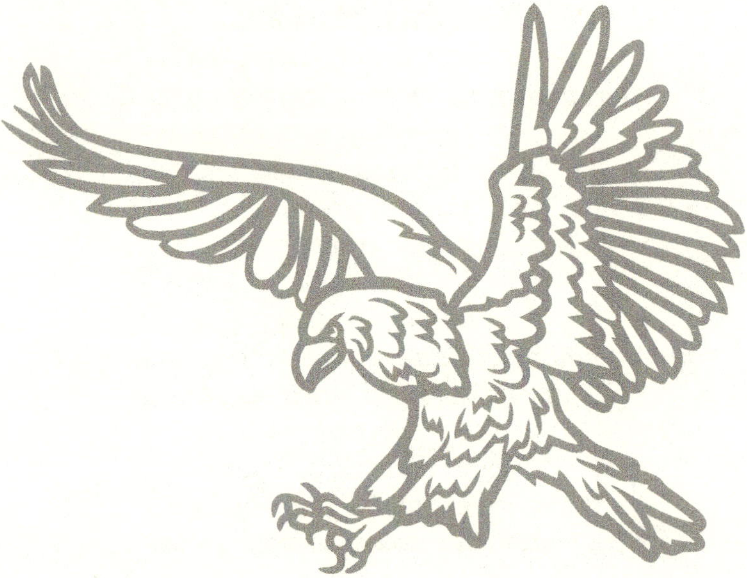

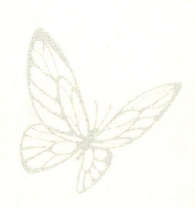

PIECES OF POETRY

Poetry lies dormant on the page and only ignites when it encounters daily life, helping us to connect with all that makes us human.

70 | *Breathe ... Alive*

Particles of Philosophy

⚛ ⚛ ⚛

Serene

*Serenity is a ship that sails
on the turbulent waves of a tempest,
on a journey to being anchored deep
in a harbour that sits still in the eye of a storm!*

🍎🍎🍎

Defiant Courage

*Courage is defying the menacing
dread of dropping off a tightrope,
but defiantly tiptoeing forward!*

⚛ ⚛ ⚛

Undying Courage

*Courage is facing imminent death by a fanged,
sharp-clawed and roaring tiger,
and battling it with your bare teeth;
for to do nothing, but crumple into a curl,
would also result in your demise.*

🍎🍎🍎

Constancy

*Integrity is maintaining a steady temperature,
whether in the glaring sunlight or the shadows
of the overhanging leaves of trees!*

Chicken Hope

Hope is a drenched chicken perched
on the lower limb of a breadfruit tree,
sitting still through a thunderstorm
and awaiting the certainty
of the sun's breaking and dawning;
so it could shake, dry and preen
its feathers!

❀ ❀ ❀

Shield of Authenticity

Authenticity exposes your spirit
to the heat of the naked truth,
but soothes the skin of your soul
from the abrasion of ungracious criticism!

🍎🍎🍎

The Taste of Truth

Unabashed confrontation could stain
the mind and mouth with a bitter residue,
but settles down sweetly in your stomach.
Fraudulent peace poisons both your body
and the soul.

❀ ❀ ❀

Insistent Splendour

Have a splendid day –
energised by the brightness of your resilience,
persistence and tenacious expectations within,
thrusting and spiralling outward:
like the radiance of the sun splintering and splattering
against the silhouettes of grey clouds!

Answers

1. *Coconut bake – A flat baked dough that is commonly eaten in Trinidad and Tobago as well as other parts of the Caribbean as an alternative to bread. Coconut bake is so named because it is flavoured with ground coconut.*

2. *Calabash gourd – The calabash is a tropical tree (Crescentia cujete) that is endemic in the Caribbean. The calabash tree produces a melon-like fruit and the word calabash is also used to refer to the gourd or the shell of the calabash fruit. Once the calabash is dried and hollowed out, it can be used for multiple purposes, including storing cosmetics, food and water and for fishing.*

3. *Dirt Oven – Dirt (or mud) ovens are made from clay which has heat-retaining properties. Dirt ovens have been used for centuries around the world. They were popular among the African population of the Caribbean. The bread, pastries and other items baked in the dirt ovens in the village of Castara in the Caribbean Island of Tobago are popular tourist attractions to this day.*

4. *Grugru Tree – A palm tree (Acrocomia sclerocarpa) that grows in the Caribbean. It has a trunk with spines, and edible nuts which are yellow when ripe.*

5.   *Cocoa House – These are wooden houses used for drying cocoa beans in the Caribbean Island of Trinidad.*

The roofs were built to slide on and off, as seen below, to allow the cocoa beans to dry in the sun.

Cocoa houses are rarely seen today.

Answers

1. *A lunar eclipse*

2. *A solar eclipse*

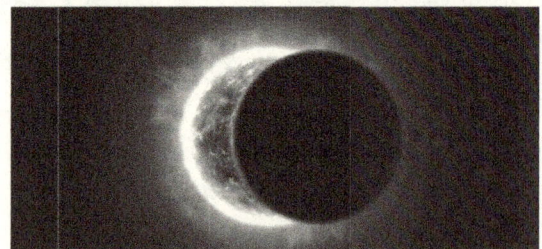

3. *A newborn*

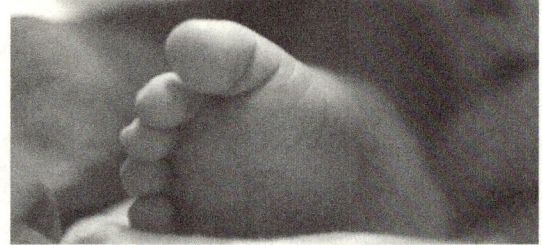

4. *A hurricane*

GLOSSARY OF TERMS

Bachac – *the name for species of leaf-cutting ants in the twin-island Republic of Trinidad and Tobago*

Beetham Dump (or Beetham Landfill) – *a major disposal site in Trinidad*

Callaloo – *a soup-like dish made with dasheen bush (i.e., taro leaves)*

Calypso – *a style of Caribbean music that originated in Trinidad*

Cascadura (or cascadu) – *a species of freshwater fish native to Trinidad and tropical Americas*

Chutney (or Chutney Soca) – *calypso incorporating English and Hindustani lyrics and accompanied by Western and Indian instruments, which is popular in Trinidad and Tobago*

Corbeaux – *a local name for vultures in Trinidad and Tobago*

Crayfish – *a freshwater crustacean*

Dasheen – *Taro, a root vegetable*

Doubles – *a sandwich made of two flatbreads (bara) which is filled with curried chickpeas, a popular street food in Trinidad and Tobago*

Karen – *an internet meme of a middle-aged and middle-class White woman whose behaviour is entitled, cantankerous and ignorant*

Monkey know not to climb – *derived from the colloquial phrase, 'Monkey know what tree to climb' used in Trinidad and Tobago, meaning people know who they could tamper or meddle with and who they should let be*

Pelau – *a popular dish in Trinidad and Tobago comprising pigeon peas, chicken or other meat, rice, fresh herbs and coconut milk*

Pothound or pothound dog – *another name for a mongrel in Trinidad and Tobago. Pothounds are known to come running when a person starts banging pots together in hopes of getting fed*

Rattans – *a discount clothing store in Trinidad which is much-maligned business enterprise*

Roti – *a flatbread sandwich filled with curried or stewed meats and vegetables which is popular in Trinidad and Tobago*

ABOUT THE AUTHOR

Deborah Boynes lives on the Caribbean Island of Trinidad, but writes poetry that appeals to persons around the globe. She is a devotee of literature for children, teenagers and adults. Deborah creates poetry that thrills you with its music and laughter, has the perfect words for the worst and best of feelings and inspires you to find the superior version of your humanity.

By day, Deborah practices financial law. She loves cooking, travelling, running, wild-life, storytelling, U.S. politics, Korean dramas and keeping up with internet memes.

Visit her:
Facebook page at:
https://www.facebook.com/profile.php?id=100089268637341
Instagram page at:
https://www.instagram.com/phoenixproductions2023/
YouTube Channel at:
https://www.youtube.com/channel/ UCP99oOJwpCUkYuI9tX67xPw

Or email her at: **pheonixproductions9@gmail.com.**

Made in United States
Orlando, FL
27 June 2025